A New True Book

THE MAYA

By Patricia C. McKissack

CHILDRENS PRESS ®

CHICAGO

Ruins of the palace at Palenque, Mexico

PHOTO CREDITS

Root Resources:
© Byron Crader—Cover, 2, 10, 40, 42
© Mary Root—20 (2 photos), 28 (right)
© Lia E. Munson—24 (left), 44 (right)

Odyssey Productions:
© Robert Frerck—6, 17, 18 (left), 21, 22, 24 (right), 26, 27, 28 (left), 32 (bottom), 35 (2 photos), 44 (left)

Nawrocki Stock Photo:
© D. Variakojis—8 (2 photos), 13 (2 photos), 14, 16, 18 (right), 31, 32 (top 2 photos), 36, 39 (2 photos), 43 (2 photos), 45

Journalism Services Inc.
© Schulman—37

Len Meents—5

Library of Congress Cataloging in Publication Data

McKissack, Pat, 1944-
   The Maya.

   (A New true book)
   Includes index.
   Summary: Describes the history, language, social classes, customs, culture, religion, and warfare of the ancient Central American civilization of the Mayas.
   1.   Mayas—Juvenile literature.   [1.   Mayas.
2.   Indians of Central America]   I.   Title.
F1435.M44   1985   972.8'01   85-9927
ISBN 0-516-01270-3   AACR2

14 15 16 R 02 01 00 99 98

TABLE OF CONTENTS

INTRODUCTION

The Mayan civilization covered what is now Belize, Guatemala, Honduras, El Salvador, and part of Mexico in Central America. Most of the Mayan land was forest and mountains.

Much of what we know about the Maya comes from Spanish records. Spaniards came to Latin

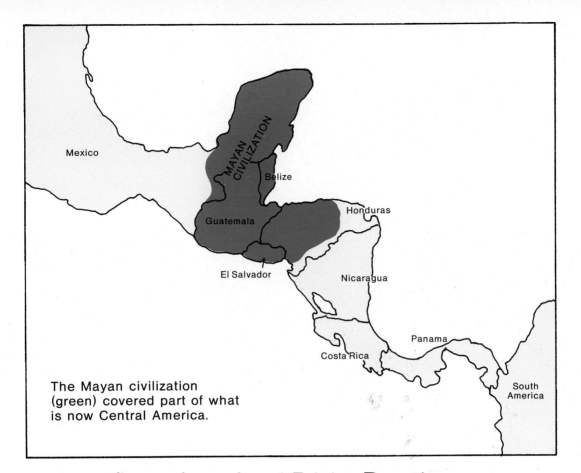

The Mayan civilization (green) covered part of what is now Central America.

America in 1511. By then the Mayan civilization was already 1,100 years old. The Maya kept records, but most of them have been destroyed or lost.

Ruins of the Mayan city and temple complex at Palenque, Mexico

MAYAN HISTORY

When the Maya-speaking people came to Central America is unknown. The classic period in Mayan history began around A.D. 320. It was a peaceful time when advances were made in knowledge, building, and farming.

The earliest known Mayan city was Uaxactún in northern Guatemala, dating back to A.D. 328.

About A.D. 700 these temples were built in Tikal, Guatemala.

Other important cities were Copán, Tikal, and Palenque. Tikal and Palenque were famous for their pyramids. One pyramid in Tikal reached over 190 feet.

Copán was a city of great learning. Scholars came there to study and work.

Mayan cities in the highlands of Guatemala were religious and political centers. Most common people lived in small villages. They went into the cities only to worship.

It is believed that over-farming helped cause the fall of this early Mayan civilization. War, famine, and changes in climate added to the fall. By 889, the Mayan cities lay in ruins.

That marked the beginning of the Yucatán

Ruins at Chichén Itzá in the Yucatán. El Caracal
is in the foreground. El Castillo is on the left,
and the Temple of the Warriors is on the right.
Chichén Itzá means "mouth of the wells of the Itzá."

period. The seat of
government then was
Chichén Itzá. The Maya
became more warlike. A
series of non-Maya-speaking
people entered their land.
These outsiders greatly
influenced the Mayan
culture.

Then in 1511 Gonzalo de Guerrero and a few other Spaniards landed on Mayan soil. Several of them were killed. Guerrero was saved by a friendly chief and was treated well. He married a Mayan woman and accepted Mayan customs. It is believed Guerrero led one of the Mayan armies against Hernando Cortés, the Spanish conqueror of Mexico.

THE MAYA PEOPLE

The Maya practiced
many different customs
and beliefs, but spoke a
common language. Over
20 forms of the Mayan
language are still spoken
today in Central America.
Ancient Mayan writing
had over eight hundred
glyphs, or carved symbols.

Mayan society was
divided into several
groups: the ruling class

The Maya wrote with glyphs, or symbols.
Glyphs were carved on stones called
stele (left) and on temple walls.

(nobility), scribes (who knew
how to write), priests,
craftsmen, and common people.

There was never a
king of all the Maya
people. Local leaders
formed the ruling class.

Carving of
Mayan priests

The priests and nobility
lived in the cities in stucco
palaces.

Priests were divided into
four special groups. The
high priest was called
Ahau Kan Mai. He led special
ceremonies and educated

the children of the nobility.

The "working priests" were called Chilan. They conducted the daily worship services. They also served as doctors and helped teach. The Nacon were in charge of sacrifices; the Chacs assisted the Nacon.

Craftsmen served the nobility. They helped build their houses and furniture. They also made the nobles' clothing, including

This carving of a male ruler wearing ceremonial dress was found in Copán, Honduras.

magnificent feathered costumes worn in special ceremonies.

The common people were farmers, hunters, and soldiers. But they all

The Maya plant corn and beans in the same field.

worked in the fields. The main crop was corn (maize). Cacao, squash, beans, and cotton also were grown. Hunters and fishermen were expected to share their catch with the rulers.

Carved stone heads are constant reminders of the Mayan civilization.

MAYAN MEN AND WOMEN

Mayan men wore plain white cotton clothing. A nobleman's clothing was embroidered with bright colors. The men wore brass and copper cuffs on their wrists and ankles. Noblemen wore gold and silver cuffs. Nose plugs and earplugs were common.

Mayan men burned their hair to form a bald spot on the top of their head. They wore their hair long. Short hair was the sign of a criminal.

Mayan women also wore plain white cotton clothing.

Clay figures of a Mayan lady (above)
and a member of the ruling class (left)

They often tattooed the
upper half of their bodies.
Women parted their hair in
the middle and braided it.
The noblewomen wore
elaborate jewelry.

20

Governor's palace in the Yucatán

Mayan women served
in government.
Both men and women
filed their teeth and
inserted plates into
their lips for special
occasions.

In this carving of a Mayan priest, you can see the head shape that the Maya considered beautiful.

GROWING UP MAYAN

Four or five days after a Mayan child was born, the mother strapped the baby between two boards. This was done to flatten and lengthen the head—a sign of beauty to the Maya.

Crossed eyes were also considered beautiful. A baby born with naturally crossed eyes was believed to be blessed by the spirits.

To make a baby's eyes cross, the mother fastened a small object to the baby's hair so that it hung just to the tip of the nose.

So that no hair grew on the face, mothers scalded their babies' faces with hot rags.

Today the Maya do not change their appearance to fit their ancestors' idea of beauty.

Although these practices seem cruel to us today, Mayan parents loved their children very much. In their culture, they were making their babies beautiful.

Children were taught by their parents. Formal education was available only to nobles and priests.

MARRIAGE AND CUSTOMS

A Mayan man was married at the age of twenty. His parents picked a bride from their village. They asked a priest to bless the marriage and choose a lucky day for the wedding. The groom's father gave the bride's parents a gift. That sealed the marriage agreement.

The wedding "ceremony" was a big feast. Afterward,

The typical Mayan home has a thatched roof and a door, but no windows.

the new husband moved to
his father-in-law's house
and worked there for
seven years. Then he and
his wife could move to
their own house.

Each family was allowed
to use a small plot of land

Beekeepers harvest honey

to grow fruits and
vegetables. Families helped
one another to plant and
harvest. Each family kept
bees for honey and raised
turkeys and ducks.

Corn (maize) was the
Maya's main food. The women

The Maya still grind corn (above) and live in houses with thatched roofs (right).

soaked the kernels in lime and water overnight. In the morning they ground the corn. Many dishes were made from corn. Stews were made from fish, fowl, and vegetables.

A Mayan house was a one-room stucco hut with a thatched roof, no windows, and one door. Inside was a large room with a sleeping area and a working area. Cooking was done outdoors.

The Maya loved company. A visitor was expected to bring a "greeting gift" to the host. Quarrels resulted when the Maya drank too much honey wine. Family feuds were common.

MAYAN ART, MUSIC, AND DANCE

The Maya loved to dance. During ceremonies and festivals the men gathered in a circle and two dancers performed in the center. Women were not included.

The Maya's favorite musical instrument was a drum made from a hollow log and skins. They also

A young boy playing the marimba in Guatemala

played gongs, flutes, and whistles.

A favorite Maya game was *pok-a-tok*. The object of the game was to drive a rubber ball through a

Women spin (above left) and weave cloth (above right) for sale in the marketplace. This Mayan mosaic plate (right) is displayed at the Museum of Anthropology in Mexico City.

ring located in the middle of the court. The players could use only their feet, legs, and hips.

The Maya painted murals on every available wall and sculpted statues in wood, stone, and metals. Their basket and cloth weaving was magnificent. They also worked with gold and silver.

RELIGION

The Maya believed the world was created by many spirits. At some time, these spirits spoke the name *earth* and it appeared. Man was created from mud, but was so weak he was destroyed by a flood. Then the spirits sent twins, who conquered evil. The twins were believed to be the

Carvings of a Chac,
a Mayan rain spirit

ancestors of the Maya
people.

The Maya worshiped
hundreds of spirits. Most
of them were nature
spirits. The Maya sacrificed
birds and other small

animals to these spirits.

The major celebration took place during Mol, the month when all the spirits were honored. The Warriors' Feast and the New Year were also special times.

Each celebration was marked by feasting,

The Maya threw offerings into the Well of Sacrifice at Chichén Itzá.

The Temple of the Warriors at Chichén Itzá

dancing, and sacrifices
to the spirits.

The Mayan people were
very careful. When a person
died, a priest had to
purify the house. Bad
spirits were thought to
be the cause of most
sickness and death.

THE MAYAN CALENDAR

The Mayan calendar
was amazingly accurate.
It had 365 days. There were
eighteen months of twenty
days each. The remaining
five days were "unlucky
days." No activities went
on during this time.

There was also a 260-day
calendar used to plan
daily life. Priests studied
the stars and decided

Market day in a small town in Guatemala (left). Masked figures (right) recall the Spanish invasion of Mayan lands.

which days were lucky
and which were unlucky.
No Maya took a trip,
planted a crop, or married
on an "unlucky day."

Mayan temple ruins at Palenque, Mexico

The Maya also had a
lunar calendar based on
the cycles of the moon.
This calendar told them
when to plant and harvest.

WARFARE

Until the Spaniards
came, the Maya were
among the mightiest
people in the area. The
Maya fought one another
from time to time, but
joined forces when
threatened by an outside
enemy.

In battle the Maya used
bows and arrows, spears,
and blowguns. Soldiers
also used wooden swords,
copper axes, and short

This Chac-Mool, was once used to hold a bowl during sacrifices at the Temple of the Warriors at Chichén Itzá.

lances. War paint was used to frighten the enemy, as was loud shouting and hissing.

Important prisoners were sacrificed to honor the ancestor of a town.

THE MAYA TODAY

Today, the Maya practice Christianity as well as their ancestral religion. They no longer flatten their babies' heads and cross their eyes.

This mother and child and the two boys standing in front of an ancient stone head are descendants of the Maya.

Rural school in the Yucatán
(above) and a woman selling
vegetables at the market (right)

Most women no longer
tattoo their bodies.

But the Maya still speak
Mayan languages and follow
many of their old customs.

44

Pigs and piglets are sold at market.

The Maya today grow many
of the same crops, enjoy the
same foods, and perform
the same colorful dances that
their ancestors did long ago.

WORDS YOU SHOULD KNOW

ancestor(AN • sess • ter) — a person from whom one is descended, usually many generations back

blowgun(BLOH • gun) — a tube through which a dart is blown, used as a weapon

civilization(siv • uh • luh • ZAY • shun) — a high stage of culture developed over a period of time

courtyard(KORT • yard) — an open space enclosed by a building

famine(FAM • un) — a shortage of food; starvation

glyphs(GLIFFS) — pictures that stand for words or syllables; a kind of writing

lance(LANTS) — a weapon consisting of a spear with a sharp, pointed end

mural(MYOOR • ul) — a painting done directly on a wall

nobility(no • BIL • uht • ee) — the people of the highest class in a country or civilization

priest(PREEST) — a man who performs religious rites

purify(PYOOR • uh • fy) — to rid of bad spirits; to make pure

pyramid(PIR • uh • mid) — a structure of stone or stone and earth that has four sides that meet in a point at the top

sacrifice(SAK • ruh • fice) — to kill an animal and offer it to a spirit

scribe(SKRYB) — a person who knows how to write

stucco(STUHK • oh) — a material used for covering walls, made of concrete and sand

INDEX

About the Author

Patricia C. McKissack and her husband, Fredrick, are freelance writers, editors, and teachers of writing. They are the owners and operators of All-Writing Services, located in Clayton, Missouri. Ms. McKissack, an award-winning editor, published author, and experienced educator, has taught writing at several St. Louis colleges and universities, including Lindenwood College, the University of Missouri at St. Louis, and Forest Park Community College.

Since 1975, Ms. McKissack has published numerous magazine articles and stories for juvenile and adult readers. She has also conducted educational and editorial workshops throughout the country for a number of organizations, businesses, and universities.

Patricia McKissack is the mother of three teenage sons. They all live in a large remodeled inner-city home in St. Louis. Aside from writing, which she considers a hobby as well as a career, Ms. McKissack likes to take care of her many plants.